Lillie La

Her life in words and pictures

By Jeremy Birkett and John Richardson

Blandford Press, Poole, Dorset
in association with **Rupert Shuff Ltd.** and the **Société Jersiaise.**

First published in Great Britain 1979.
First published in this edition in 1979 by Blandford Press
Ltd., Link House, West Street, Poole, Dorset, BH15 1LL.

ISBN 0 7137 1073 X

 Approved by the Société Jersiaise.

Design and Artwork by John Clark Studio, Bournemouth, Dorset.

Extra Photography by Studio 4, Bournemouth, Dorset.

Typesetting by Shaun Ryan, Bournemouth, Dorset.

Printed by Megaron Press Ltd., Bournemouth, Dorset.

Acknowledgements

Our grateful thanks to all those who assisted in the compilation of this book, especially: Mr. R. W. Higginbottom, M.A., A.M.A., Curator and Mr. G. Drew, Assistant Curator, of the Jersey Museum, Mrs. J. Stevens, M.B.E., Members of the Committee of the Société Jersiaise, Mr. H. T. Porter, Mrs. Colin McFadyean, Mr. David Butler, Mr. Charles Clegg, Mr. Jeremy Marks, The Radio Times Hulton Picture Library, The Raymond Mander and Joe Mitchenson Theatre Collection, the Bournemouth Evening Echo, London Weekend Television, The Guardian, John Clark Studio, Sharon Ward and Linda Norrie.

Jeremy Birkett & John Richardson, March 1979.

Foreword

You are in for many surprises as you read this brief biography of my grandmother, Lillie Langtry. Perhaps you will be shocked, but perhaps also it will occur to you that she was a woman in advance — by many years — of her time, in her adoption of the principals of "Women's Lib". She was a theatre owner, actress-manager of her own company, planned all her tours of America, was a racehorse owner and member of the all-male Jockey Club as "Mr. Jersey"; she owned a large, sea-going yacht, which she raced, and a ranch in America. Infinitely resilient in the face of disaster, her maxim was always: "Let us not fuss please", delivered (according to the late A. E. Matthews, a distinguished British actor who was once a young member of her Company) in a voice calculated to quell all doubts.

Jeanne-Marie, her only daughter and my mother, had an unhappy childhood, spent mostly in the company of the servants in Lillie's London house, or in hotel rooms on tour with her in the United States. She never went to school, and her early years were an influence for the rest of her life.

Lillie's name was not mentioned in our household and I met her only once when I was eleven and she was in the last years of her life. I have happy memories of the afternoon we spent together in her London hotel; to me she seemed a perfect Granny. Asked what I wanted for my birthday, I replied: "a bicycle", and one arrived a few days later "with Lady de Bathe's compliments". Time had mellowed Lillie but my mother was unrelenting and would not receive her. All too vivid in my mother's memory were the stories my grandmother told her about her parentage, before finally admitting the truth on the eve of her marriage and making a typically forthright comment: "Wouldn't you rather have a man like that for a father than a drunken Irish sot?" This was not a remark which did anything to endear her mother to Jeanne-Marie, but I, one generation removed, can only say that I am proud to think that, flowing in my veins, is a stream of blood which stems from one of England's greatest and most ill-used servants, Prince Louis of Battenberg, the man whom Lillie loved and who loved her and would have married her had it been possible.

Mary Malcolm, Lillie Langtry's grand-daughter.

Contents

List of Illustrations

Continued overleaf.

List of Illustrations (continued)

Lillie Langtry's birth certificate

EXTRAIT DU REGISTRE DES NAISSANCES

De la Paroisse de SAINT SAUVEUR , Ile de Jersey.

[PAGE 37]

No.	Date et lieu de la naissance	Prénoms s'il y en a	Sexe	Nom et Prénom du Père	Nom et famille et Prénom de la Mère	Etat ou Profession du Père	Naissance, Description et Domicile de l'Informateur	Date de l'Enregistrement	Signature de l'Enregistreur	Nom de Baptême s'il a été ajouté après l'Inscription de Naissance
361	Treizième Octobre 1853. Rectorat	Emilie Charlotte	Fille	William Corbet Le Breton	Emilie Davis Martin	Doyen de l'Isle de Jersey et Recteur de la Paroisse de Saint Sauveur	William Corbet Le Breton, Père de l'Enfant, Rectorat.	Vingt-huitième Octobre 1853.	Joseph Gregg, Enregistreur.	

Je certifie par ces présentes que c'est ici un Extrait fidèle du Registre des Naissances de la Paroisse de Saint Sauveur , en l'Ile de Jersey.

Témoin mon seing, ce 4e jour de Septembre 1965 .

J. H. Coutanche Enregistreur.

"She had dewy violet eyes, a complexion like a peach. How can words convey the vitality, the glow, the amazing charm that made this fascinating woman the centre of any group she entered?"

This tribute, written by Daisy, Countess of Warwick, some fifty years after their first encounter, gives us as clear an insight as any into the true magic of that phenomenon of the Victorian and Edwardian era, Lillie Langtry, the Jersey Lily.

I. Her Childhood

Born on the 13th October, 1853 in the Old Rectory at St. Saviour in the lovely Island of Jersey, Lillie was christened Emilie Charlotte Le Breton. She was the only daughter of the Very Reverend William Corbet Le Breton, Dean of Jersey and his wife Emilie. The Le Bretons had established themselves in Jersey in the Channel Islands by the thirteenth century, the family believed a Le Breton fought in the battle of Hastings in 1066 alongside William the Conqueror, whose domain included Jersey. This ancestor was supposedly pictured in the famous Bayeux Tapestry. Emilie, nicknamed 'Lillie', went one day to see the Tapestry but was very disappointed not to be able to discern any family likeness in the woven face of the helmeted hero!

Lillie's mother, Emilie le Breton (née Martin).

Lillie had six brothers, all but one older than she. It is not surprising, then, that she grew into an incorrigible tom-boy, joining in the never-ending pranks that her brothers played on various people. Any discovery of mischievous goings-on, whether it were a sudden outbreak of missing doorknockers in the Parish or the nightly appearance of ghostly apparitions in St. Saviour's churchyard, was blamed on the Dean's children, usually with some justification!

Her brothers impressed upon Lillie the handicaps of not being a boy. They would not put up with a silly little girl spoiling things for them. "You must look at things from a boy's point of view," they would say.

Her father, William Corbet le Breton, Dean of Jersey.

Lillie, as a young girl.

Inevitably, these childhood experiences imbued Lillie with a toughness of spirit and the resolve throughout her life never to allow herself the weak luxury of tears.

Evidence of Lillie's blossoming beauty could be seen at an early age and was certainly the undoing of a dashing young army officer, Lieut. Longley, son of the Archbishop of Canterbury. He had seen Lillie several times riding her pony on the golden sands of Island beaches in the early morning sunshine, and had immediately fallen in love with this angelic vision. He approached the Dean to ask for her hand in marriage, only to be told: "But surely you must know, my daughter is only fourteen years of age . . ." The heartbroken Lieutenant left the island shortly after, feeling somewhat foolish.

A family portrait, taken about 1864, with her parents and one of her six brothers.

Lillie very soon became accepted as the most beautiful girl in Jersey, and there were naturally many suitors. However, she had hopes and ambitions that stretched far beyond the shores of this quiet, picturesque little island.

At the age of twenty, she saw her opportunity. A wealthy young Irish widower had arrived in Jersey and become well acquainted with her brothers. His name was Edward Langtry.

The Old Rectory, St. Saviour, Jersey — Lillie's childhood home.

2. Edward Langtry

Edward and Mrs. Langtry shortly after their marriage.

This young man, of independent means, but with no profession had a luxurious yacht the "Red Gauntlet". His family's wealth had originated from grandfather George, Belfast's largest shipowner.

Whether true love ever really blossomed between the two was doubtful. Lillie perhaps thought that she loved him, but the attraction was more likely to have been the "Red Gauntlet" on which she spent many exhilarating hours. Furthermore, this beautiful yacht represented her passage to the big wide world outside her Island.

The wedding took place in St. Saviour's Parish Church on 9th March, 1874, the Dean performing the service, perhaps with some understandable misgivings in his heart. After an informal wedding breakfast at the Royal Jersey Yacht Club, Edward and Lillie sailed away in the "Red Gauntlet". Lillie felt an almost overpowering sense of exhilaration that, at last, she was going to taste some of the delights of adulthood that she felt awaited her.

Noirmont Manor in Jersey was the first home of the newlyweds, but Lillie's impatience to explore life further afield soon took them away from the Island. Edward owned a large house overlooking Southampton Water called "Cliffe Lodge", and when they moved there Lillie felt, with some satisfaction, that they were halfway to her target destination — London.

While at Southampton, Lillie contracted typhoid and for many weeks lay dangerously ill. Edward engaged the best local doctor available, a Dr. Lewis, and a nurse to watch over her day and night. When finally the raging fever had subsided, and Lillie was convalescing, the doctor advised his patient that a change of air was necessary. During the fight to save her life, the doctor had become uncommonly fond of his beautiful patient. This must have had a bearing on the fact that Edward, under the doctor's persuasion, begrudgingly agreed to take Lillie to London.

Lillie at the time of her first marriage.

Oscar Wilde, a close friend of Lillie. He once bought a white amaryllis for a few pence from Covent Garden market and walked through London with it, saying to onlookers: "I am carrying this to Mrs. Langtry. Would you not gladly change places?" ▷

3. London Society

To Lillie, London was the hub of the universe. It embodied all her dreams and hopes of life. She was aware of the squalor and poverty which she deplored, that was so visibly prevalent in many parts of London a century ago, but was determined to concentrate all her energies on making an impression on the high Society of which she wished to become a part.

The Langtry's first home was in Eaton Place, in London's fashionable Belgravia. They did not have long to wait before their first taste of the pleasurable life in Society. A friend of her father's, the seventh Viscount Ranelagh, whom Lillie had met in Jersey, arranged for them to be invited to a reception at the opulent home of Sir John and Lady Sebright in Lowndes Square. Wearing a very simple figure-hugging black dress, in mourning for her beloved younger brother Reggie, who died as a result of a riding accident, the young Lillie made a profound impression on the distinguished gathering, which comprised many of the outstanding artists of the time.

By the end of the evening, she had already been sketched by Frank Miles, asked to sit for a portrait by Millais, and established herself as the latest talking point of Society. Over the next few days, she and Edward received a flood of invitations to dine, take tea, attend a reception or a ball. Lillie had arrived.

In their early months in London, Edward and Lillie used to take a stroll in Hyde Park, that beautiful stretch of greenery in central London. At that time, the Park was the setting for grandiose display, the fashionable set taking the air on horseback and in every type of carriage, from four-in-hands to racing turn-outs.

Sarah Bernhardt,
the famous stage actress and inspiration to
Lillie in her own theatrical career.

William Ewart Gladstone, Britain's Prime
Minister, a good friend and well respected
by Lillie.

An accomplished horsewoman herself, Lillie longed to be a part of the elegant daily parade, to demonstrate to those who thronged to watch that Mrs. Langtry had truly secured her position in Society. She did not have long to wait. One day in the park she was introduced to a Mr. Moreton Frewen, the son of one of England's largest landowners. This wealthy young man, smitten with the charms of the lovely Mrs. Langtry, presented her with a magnificent show-hack named "Redskin". From that day on, Lillie caused a great sensation as she rode in Rotten Row. Spectators would climb upon chairs to see the Jersey Lily ride by at the fashionable hour, followed closely by an escort of male admirers; "Langtry's Lancers", as they were popularly known.

Soon after arriving in London, she had caught her first glance of the Prince of Wales as he rode through the Park with his aides; imagine her satisfaction therefore, not many months later, when the admiring onlookers cheered and bowed as the Prince rode past in all his finery, accompanied by the flawless Mrs. Langtry.

Her husband, however, found the ensuing months and years of endless socialising both bewildering and tiresome. A shy, introverted man, he found his escape more and more in the solitude of fishing and drink.

Prince Louis of Battenberg, Edward VII's favourite nephew, and father of Lillie's daughter, Jeanne-Marie.

Prince Paul Esterhazy of Hungary, who unsuccessfully proposed marriage to Lillie.

4. Portraits

The young Frank Miles' soft and life-like sketches of Lillie were soon on sale in shops all over London and she became acknowledged as the loveliest of the "Professional Beauties", as the most decorative ladies of London Society were then known.

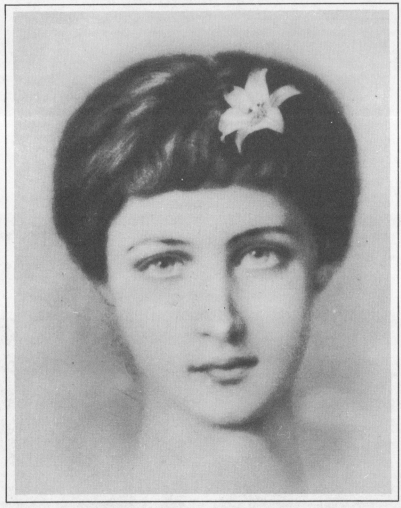

Frank Miles' drawing of Lillie which was removed from the bedroom wall of Prince Leopold by his disapproving mother, Queen Victoria.

Without sufficient income from Edward to afford the opulent gowns of the other ladies, Lillie was content to wear the same black dress, maintaining her mourning for her brother. This became almost her trade mark, and Millais insisted that she should wear it when she sat for her portrait.

The result showed a gentle, pensive girl, holding a crimson lily. Named "A Jersey Lily", this was one of Lillie's favourite portraits of herself, capturing so accurately as it did her beautiful complexion. The painting was hung with great success in the Royal Academy, where it had to be roped around to avoid damage by the crowds who thronged to see it. It was nominated as the picture of the year on three occasions, in 1879, 1890 and again, thirty years later in 1920. The painting was purchased by the States of Jersey and it now hangs in the Art Gallery at Fort Regent in St. Helier.

Another famous portrait, showing Lillie in a gorgeous golden gown, was painted by Sir Edward Poynter, P.R.A. and can also be seen in Jersey, in the Museum of the Société Jersiaise at St. Helier. She loaned it for some time to Oscar Wilde, a close and adoring friend who gave her much support and advice during her early years in London.

Other notable painters who tried to capture her elusive beauty on canvas were George Frederick Watts, who painted her in "The Dean's Daughter", Edward Burne-Jones who eventually persuaded Lillie to pose for him in "The Golden Stair" where she appears twice, once in full face and once in profile, standing on the lower steps. Burne-Jones also painted her in "Dame Fortune", a painting which used to hang in the study of Arthur Balfour, who became Prime Minister in 1902. Amongst works by James Whistler were two etchings of Lillie entitled "Effie Deans" and "At The Toilette".She also posed for Millais in a painting of "Effie Deans". Frederick Leighton sculpted a marble bust of her, which is said to have been commissioned by the Prince of Wales.

Of all the artists, however, Sir John Millais remained her favourite and she spent many happy hours in his studio overlooking Hyde Park. He told her she was the most exasperating subject he had ever painted — that she looked just beautiful for about fifty five out of sixty minutes, but for five minutes in every hour she was amazing.

The "Triptych" by Frank Miles which was put on sale in London shops, spreading her fame as a professional beauty.

Drawing by Frank Miles, showing the famous "Langtry Knot".

"A Jersey Lily", by Sir John Millais, P.R.A. now hanging in the Art Gallery at Fort Regent, Jersey.

MRS. LANGTRY.

*The portrait by Sir Edward Poynter P.R.A., which
now hangs in the Jersey Museum.*

"The Dean's Daughter"
by George Frederick Watts.

A self-portrait of Watts.

Lillie wearing the little black hat, thought
to have been drawn for a charity fête.

As Kate Hardcastle in
"She Stoops to Conquer"

5. The Prince of Wales

London Society took its cue from "The Marlborough Set", as the Prince of Wales' own chosen group of friends were popularly known. Although Heir to the Throne, Bertie, as he was familiarly called, was excluded from playing any useful role in the affairs of the Monarchy by his mother, Queen Victoria, who disapproved of his rumbustious lifestyle. He thus spent much of his time hunting, shooting and being entertained at the residences of his many friends up and down the country. His beautiful Danish born wife Alexandra had long since resigned herself to her husband's ways, and she maintained great poise and dignity in turning a blind eye to his affairs with other women.

Inevitably, Bertie came to hear of this new beauty, known as the *Jersey Lily*, who was taking London by storm. Through subtle manoeuverings on the part of his equerries, Sir Allen Young and Lord Suffield, Lillie was introduced to the future King of England at a discreet dinner party. By the twinkle in his piercing blue eyes, she knew that she had passed the test. The Prince was bowled over by her natural beauty and charmed by her intelligent and well-informed conversation.

So began a long and warm relationship. They were two of a kind, suited to each other's needs. Lillie had a strong personality and refused to be subservient, and it was this quality in her which gained Bertie's respect and his admiration for her beauty. She became his first acknowledged mistress, and to the astonishment of all observers, also developed a respectful and affectionate friendship with the Princess Alexandra, who seemed to feel that this time, Bertie had, at least, chosen a woman of intelligence and learning.

Through the Prince's influence, Lillie was presented to Queen Victoria at Buckingham Palace. Wearing a breathtaking ivory gown, with a long train, and at her head three huge white ostrich plumes — the Prince of Wales' own personal emblem — she must have impressed the Queen with her beauty and her audacity as she curtsied deeply and kissed the hand of the small, black-clad monarch; Victoria said not a word.

Bertie was determined to build a house that could be their own personal retreat. A site was chosen on the sandstone cliffs overlooking the sea in the beautiful south-coast resort of Bournemouth. The foundation stone bore the date 1877 and Lillie's initials 'E.L.L.', Emilie Le Breton Langtry. "The Red House", as she named it, was warm and inviting, reflecting Lillie's influence, as well as her imprint. On a south wall was inscribed a simple message: "Dulce Domum", (A sweet home); and hidden in the pale oak carving of the mantlepiece, again her initials 'E.L.L.'. There was also a touch of humour the Prince and

Bertie, Prince of Wales. 1876.

Lillie clearly shared. Along the wall of the dining room was written: "They say — What say they? Let them say." and in the hallway: "And yours, my friend." On the outside wall of the suite of rooms reserved for the Prince, were inscribed the words "Stet Fortuna Domus" — (may fortune attend those who dwell here). Also exclusively for his benefit, a tiny hatch was built high in the wall of the dining room, through which he could inspect the company, unseen before descending to dinner.

The house stands in its own grounds today in Derby Road, its originality preserved as an hotel, *"The Langtry Manor"*.

Though the Prince of Wales' attentions were inevitably distracted by other emerging beauties as the years passed, his friendship with Lillie continued till the end of his days, and she still used to visit Bertie and Alexandra when in London, even after Bertie had become King Edward VII on the death of his mother in 1901.

Lillie had developed a close and loving relationship with the Prince's nephew, Prince Louis of Battenberg, a handsome young British naval officer. Though unable to marry him because of her husband's refusal to agree to a divorce, Lillie bore him a daughter called Jeanne-Marie. To avoid any possible scandal this little girl was brought up to believe her mother was her aunt and addressed her always as "Ma tante". She was ten before she discovered the truth, but not until she was eighteen and engaged to be married did she find out who her true father was.

Jeanne-Marie married Ian Malcolm, a politician, and she later became Lady Malcolm M.B.E.. They had a beautiful home, "Poltalloch", on Scotland's Mull of Kintyre, and a family of four children; three boys, and a girl who became one of the B.B.C.'s first T.V. announcers, Mary Malcolm, now Mrs. Colin McFadyean.

The "Crow's Nest", on the Crichel estate, reputed to be a favourite meeting place of Lillie and the Prince of Wales, during his visits to Crichel House, in Dorset, then the home of Lord Alington.

"The Red House", Bournemouth, built for Lillie by Bertie, Prince of Wales.

Crichel House, Dorset, home of Lord Alington, a wealthy patron of the theatre.

6. Her Theatrical Career

With her husband Edward continually away on his fishing trips, and with money becoming a serious problem, Lillie turned her attention to some means of supporting herself, not wishing to continue to rely on the generosity of the Prince.

Lillie, in "A Fair Encounter", her stage debut at the Town Hall, Twickenham, 1881.

"Still as a barmaid"

Lillie Langtry

As Kate Hardcastle, the barmaid, in "She Stoops To Conquer". Her ironic comment and signature can be seen below.

Since seeing performances by the Parisian Comédie Française tour in England, and becoming well acquainted with the leading lady, Sarah Bernhardt, Lillie had developed a keen interest in the theatre. She was greatly influenced by the "divine Sarah", as her London public called her. In her autobiography, Lillie described the great influence that Mlle. Bernhardt had had on her and referred to the 'transcendent genius' of this great actress.

It was a lady named Henrietta Labouchère, a retired actress, who eventually persuaded Lillie to take up acting. In her first play "A Fair Encounter", performed at Twickenham Town Hall, she played Lady Clara, and her first experience on the 'Boards' was not without incident: "when I found myself on the diminutive stage, my mind became a blank. Alas! not a word of the opening soliloquy could I remember. There I stood, a forced smile on my lips and a bunch of roses in my arms, without the vestige of an idea what was to happen next." Eventually she regained her composure.

However, after this first, somewhat testing experience, Lillie's theatrical career blossomed with the support and enthusiasm of her friends, including the Prince of Wales. Her second performance, as Kate Hardcastle, in "She Stoops To Conquer", was a great success, and Lillie became a professional member of the Bancroft Company.

Her fortunes prospered, and before long, Lillie founded her own acting Company, with which she undertook a highly successful provincial tour with four plays: 'Ours', 'She Stoops To Conquer', playing Rosalind in 'As You Like It' and 'Peril'.

She was now established as both a notable beauty and an acclaimed actress, drawing full houses wherever she performed. It was time, she decided, to try her luck in the United States, a place which fascinated her from all that she had read and heard about it. Her guide and mentor, Henrietta Labouchère, accompanied her, to the disgust of Henrietta's politician husband, who was fond of handing out a little sarcastic wit when the women were rehearsing. He wrote a poem which did not please Lillie overmuch. It was published in 'Truth' magazine on their departure to the States:

"Sing of Mrs. Langtry, a lady full of grace,
Four-and-twenty sonnets written to her face;
Now that face is public, and we can also sing,
Is she not a dainty dame, and worthy of a King?"

Lillie's reputation as one of the most beautiful women in England, and the publicly acknowledged mistress of the Prince of Wales, Heir to the Throne, preceded her across the Atlantic. Her reception was ecstatic. Following the example of Sarah Bernhardt, she took a suite at the Albemarle Hotel overlooking Madison Square. She was due to open within a few days at Abbey's Park Theatre and the boxes and stalls for the premiere had been auctioned for the then magnificent sum of twenty thousand dollars. On the night of the performance, disaster struck. Fire broke out in the theatre and as Lillie watched, the whole building was gutted. All that remained — a sign high above the roof bearing the words, "Mrs. Langtry".

Another theatre was very soon hired, and Lillie opened before her American public in the comedy-drama "An Unequal Match" by Tom Taylor. Her description of the event: "The evening was memorable, the audience enthusiastic, and the floral tributes showered on me were a revelation."

In "The Degenerates", a play which aroused great excitement when performed in America.

As Hester Grazebrook in "An Unequal Match", by Tom Taylor, in 1882.

In "Peril" at the Prince of Wales Theatre in 1885.

33

As Rosalind, in "As You Like It", 1889.

MRS LANGTRY COPYRIGHT

As Marie Antoinette.

As Blanche Haye in "Ours", a comedy by Thomas Robertson.

In "Pygmalion and Galatea"   "Mademoiselle Mars".

A scene from the play "Princess George".

As Pauline, in "The Lady of Lyons", a sketch by W. G. Baxter.

Front page of "The Bystander", 29th April, 1908, at the time of her latest production "A Fearful Joy", her first appearance as Lady de Bathe.

The Bystander, April 29, 1908

Each Number of "The Bystander" contains
AN ACCIDENT INSURANCE POLICY FOR £2,000

The BYSTANDER.

Sport, Pastimes & Travel.

Art, Literature & the Drama.

No. 230 —Vol. XVIII. [Registered at the G.P.O. as a Newspaper.]   Wednesday, April 29, 1908   [Price 6d. By Post, 6½d.

Photo   Lafayette

THE LATEST PHOTOGRAPH OF MRS. LANGTRY (LADY DE BATHE)

She is now playing in "A Fearful Joy," with which she opened her season at the Haymarket, this being her first appearance in
London since her husband succeeded to the Baronetcy.   The reports regarding valuable discoveries of gold on her Californian estates
have proved to be without foundation

Lillie, Lady de Bathe, in the one film that she made, "His Neighbour's Wife", in 1913.

As "Cleopatra", 1890.

7. Experiences in America

Lillie toured with her company throughout the United States, capturing the hearts of the American public wherever she went. Her hats and dresses, even her hairstyle, were copied across the land, and "Lillie" soon became a most popular name for baby girls.

During her travels, Lillie met Freddie Gebhard, a wealthy and handsome businessman from Baltimore. He adored her, and showered her with endless extravagant gifts. But his greatest gift was to commission a special railway car for her from Colonel Mann, inventor of the Mann boudoir railway carriage.

She called the carriage the "Lalee", an old Indian word meaning 'flirt'. At a cost of a quarter of a million pounds, it had ten rooms, including a fully-serviced kitchen and every conceivable luxury to ensure comfort and peace of mind as Lillie travelled across the thousands of miles of the vast continent. With its deep blue exterior coachwork and the emblazoned wreaths of golden lilies encircling the name, Mrs. Langtry's magnificent carriage attracted great attention wherever it went. However, the 'Lalee' came to a tragic end, being totally destroyed by fire during Lillie's temporary absence one season.

At one performance in Chicago, Lillie had been seen by Judge Roy Bean, Justice of the Peace of a small southern Texan village called Vinagaroon. A forceful and ambitious man, he had established himself as the self-styled "Law West of the Pecos River". He was so taken with Lillie that he renamed the village, Langtry, and christened the saloon where he served up liquor and rough and ready justice in his capacity as both saloon-keeper and judge, the "Jersey Lilly". This saloon has been immortalised as part of the Judge Roy Bean Museum which can be seen in Langtry, Val Verde County, Texas. Although she was never to meet the Judge, Lillie did visit Langtry briefly in 1904 when the 'Lalee' was passing close by. The famous 'Judge' had died a few months earlier, but the townsfolk came out in their best attire to greet the Jersey Lily as the 'Lalee', coupled to the Southern Pacific Railway's transcontinental train, rolled to a halt. The train could wait only thirty minutes, so the Justice of the Peace, W. Dodd, and his reception committee trudged along the lines to welcome their heroine. As a gift from the town, they brought with them a huge brown bear which was tethered to the rear platform of her carriage. To Lillie's relief the bear broke loose and escaped, and in its place she was presented with the late Judge Roy Bean's revolver.

Freddie Gebhard, a close companion of Lillie in America and donor of the "Lalee".

While in America, Lillie bought a ranch of about six thousand five hundred acres in California and named it "Langtry Farms". Situated in Lake County, in the Howell Mountains, this property gave her a lot of pleasure and she wrote fondly of it in her autobiography. Circumstances, however, led her to sell it after only a short period of ownership, for about half the price she had paid for it. It is now a part of the Guenoc Ranch.

In 1884, Lillie resolved to obtain a divorce from Edward. Such action was legally possible in the States, though not in England where Edward still refused to countenance the idea of legal separation. So it was that her marriage was dissolved in Lakeport, California, on the grounds that Edward had deserted her!

The "Lalee", the luxurious railway carriage built especially for Lillie during her theatrical travels across America. Her daughter, Jeanne-Marie, accompanied her on some of these trips, as a small child.

Lillie wrote of the United States: — "The immensity of the Continent was fascinating; the excitement of being whirled over vast tracts of magnificent country from one great city to another, the novelty and comfort of railway travelling, and, above all, the warm-heartedness of the American welcome, made a strong appeal; and so it came to pass that, without losing my love for the Union Jack, I coupled with it a great affection for the Stars and Stripes. During the five consecutive years that I played in America, I fancy that I grew more familiar with the country than were most Americans, for I can hardly put my finger on any town sufficiently important to be marked on the map in which I have not played more than once . . . but, however long I may remain absent from 'The Land of the Free', the days spent there will remain shrined in my store of happy memories." Lillie Langtry was granted American citizenship on 17th July, 1887.

LAW WEST OF THE PECOS

JUDGE ROY BEAN LIVED A LIFE IN WHICH FICTION BECAME SO INTERMINGLED WITH FACT THAT HE BECAME A LEGEND WITHIN HIS LIFETIME. BASIS FOR HIS RENOWN WERE THE DECISIONS WHICH HE REACHED IN THIS BUILDING AS THE LAW WEST OF THE PECOS. COURT WAS HELD AS FREQUENTLY ON THE PORCH, SPECTATORS GROUPED ABOUT ON HORSEBACK, AS WITHIN THE BUILDING. NOR WAS BEAN ABOVE BREAKING OFF PROCEEDINGS LONG ENOUGH TO SERVE CUSTOMERS SEEKING SERVICES DISPENSED BY THE OTHER BUSINESSES CARRIED ON IN HIS COURTROOM-HOME.

THE JUDGE'S "LAW LIBRARY" CONSISTED OF A SINGLE VOLUME, AN 1879 COPY OF THE REVISED STATUTES OF TEXAS. HE SELDOM CONSULTED IT, HOWEVER, CALLING INSTEAD ON HIS OWN IDEAS ABOUT THE BRAND OF JUSTICE WHICH SHOULD APPLY. THIS HE EFFECTIVELY DISPENSED TOGETHER WITH LIBERAL QUANTITIES OF BLUFF AND BLUSTER. SINCE LANGTRY HAD NO JAIL, ALL OFFENSES WERE DEEMED FINABLE WITH BEAN POCKETING THE FINES. DRUNKEN PRISONERS OFTEN WERE CHAINED TO MESQUITE TREES IN FRONT OF THE BUILDING UNTIL THEY SOBERED UP ENOUGH TO STAND TRIAL.

BEAN REACHED A PEAK OF NOTORIETY WHEN, ON FEBRUARY 21, 1896, HE STAGED THE BANNED FITZSIMMONS-MAHER HEAVYWEIGHT TITLE FIGHT ON A SAND BAR IN THE RIO GRANDE RIVER, A STONE'S THROW FROM HIS FRONT PORCH. BY HOLDING IT ON MEXICAN TERRITORY HE OUTWITTED TEXAS RANGERS SENT TO STOP THE MATCH -- AND TURNED A HANDSOME PROFIT FOR HIS SHREWDNESS.

THIS BUILDING WAS NAMED THE "JERSEY LILLY" FOR THE FAMOUS ENGLISH ACTRESS LILLIE LANGTRY WHOM BEAN ADMIRED AND FOR WHOM HE CLAIMED TO HAVE NAMED THE TOWN. HIS LAMP FREQUENTLY BURNED INTO THE NIGHT AS HE COMPOSED LETTERS TO HER. BUT HE NEVER SAW HER SINCE HER ONLY VISIT TO LANGTRY OCCURRED IN 1904, LESS THAN A YEAR AFTER BEAN DIED.

"The Jersey Lilly Saloon", Langtry, Texas, in which Judge Roy Bean reigned supreme as saloon-keeper, justice-of-the-peace and self-styled "law west of the Pecos".

As "Lady Macbeth" in New York, 1889.

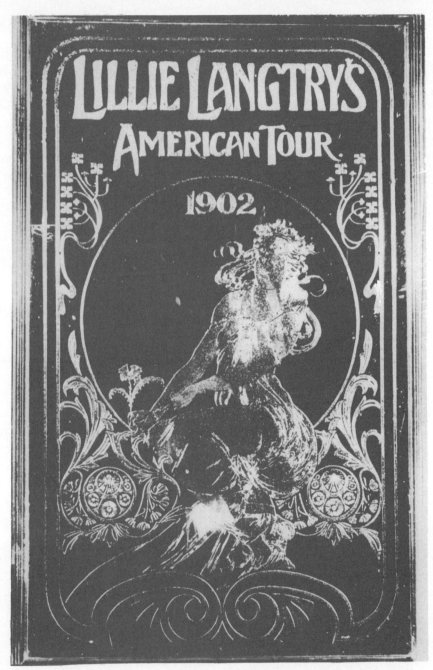

Poster of Lillie's American tour.

8. Racing Interests

On her return to England, Lillie began to develop great interest in horse racing. She tolerated the attentions and company of two flirtatious noblemen, Lord Hugh Lonsdale and Sir George Chetwynd, on account of their close involvement with the world of racing and breeding. These gentlemen provided Lillie with a very valuable insight into the excitements and ramifications of the "turf".

A third gentleman, of Scottish descent, and also with strong racing connections, became Lillie's constant escort. "Squire Abingdon" was a wealthy industrialist who owned a stable of thoroughbreds. A somewhat violent man, he had the unfortunate weakness of striking his lady friends in moments of temper, only to be consumed with deep remorse the moment the deed was done, subsequently showering the victim with extravagant gifts in atonement. It was in this way that Lillie came to own a fine two-year-old chestnut colt called 'Milford' who won his maiden race at Kempton Park.

Lillie went on to enjoy some notable successes in her racing activities, first with 'Lady Rosebery' who won, among others, the Lanark Cup and the Jockey Club Cup at Newmarket; and latterly with the famous 'Merman', whose many outstanding successes included the Cesarewitch, the Ascot Gold Cup, the Jockey Club Cup and the Goodwood Cup. As a reminder of the sadder side of her married life, forty-eight hours after 'Merman's' victory in the Cesarewitch, Lillie learned of her husband's death. She had supported him financially ever since their parting, but Edward Langtry had finally died alone in a Chester asylum.

'Squire Abingdon' also purchased a magnificent two hundred and twenty foot steam yacht for Lillie, named "The White Ladye", in which, on one occasion, at least, she visited Jersey.

Merman Cottage, bought by Lillie, at Beaumont, Jersey, Channel Islands.

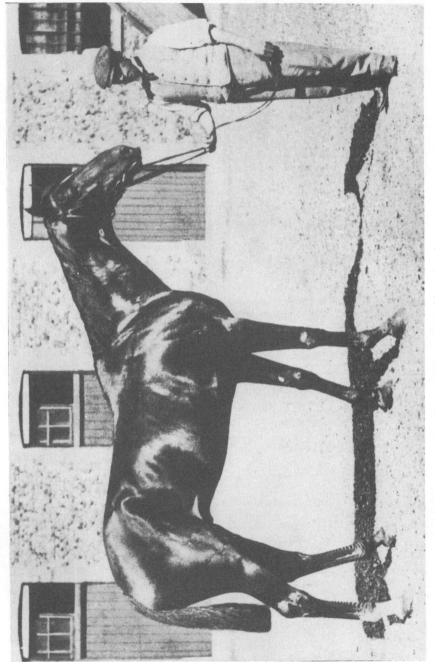

The famous "Merman" in his racing days.

9. Lady de Bathe

Her appetite for vigorous and youthful pursuits led Lillie to marry again in later life, once more in St. Saviour's Church, Jersey in 1899. Nineteen years her junior, Hugo de Bathe was a mild, likeable man who, on his father's death, inherited the Baronetcy and became Sir Hugo, so that Lillie achieved perhaps her final social ambition by becoming Lady de Bathe.

She had reason to feel a sense of satisfaction as she looked back on a life in which she had achieved all things for which she had striven. Famous artists of the day had clamoured to capture her on canvas; Oscar Wilde had slept all night on her doorstep while creating his poetic offering 'The New Helen — formerly of Troy, now of London'; the future King of England had loved her and remained her close friend until he died in 1910; she had made a successful career in the theatre; had owned yachts, a ranch, her own railway carriage, a string of fine race horses and many lovely homes.

She had known Royalty, landed gentry, famous artists, leaders of Society and well-known politicians. The British Prime Minister, Gladstone, for whom she had a high regard, had said to her when she was a young woman: "In your professional career, you will receive attacks, personal and critical, just and unjust. Bear them, never reply, and, above all, never rush into print to explain or defend yourself." Lillie was to follow this astute advice throughout her life.

She was not only a notable beauty, but in her day a woman of exceptional learning and reading. Furthermore, she was always well-informed on contemporary topics, and was, thus, throughout her life an excellent conversationalist. She usually looked her best wherever she was and whatever she was doing, maintaining always her lovely complexion, no doubt perpetuated by the cold bath she frequently took at the start of the day.

Of all the many men who had admired and loved her, it is believed that one in particular remained closest to her heart. His name was Arthur Jones, a boyhood friend of her brother Reggie. He remained in Jersey to manage his family farm but often visited Lillie in London during her early years. Their deep love for one another, however, was possibly frustrated by their widely-differing lifestyles.

Her last days were spent in the sunshine of Monaco, where she satisfied her competitive urges with the occasional flutter at the casino. It was in Monaco that she died, on February 12th 1929, at the age of 75, in her pretty villa "Le Lys", on the edge of the cliff facing the beautiful Mediterranean.

Lillie's daughter Jeanne-Marie and granddaughter Mary, dressed in the tartan of her husband, Ian Malcolm's clan, taken in the mid-1920's.

So let us end the story of this remarkable woman in the words of David Butler, writer of the highly successful television series, "Lillie":
"A creator and setter of fashions, in her attitudes to social conventions, clothes, sex, the paraphernalia of living, she was at least fifty years ahead of her time. She was no suffragette, she considered them sadly unfeminine, but in a male dominated society she stood for the right of women to lead an independent, unshackled life. No woman ever did so with more notable success."

Fittingly, her body was returned to Jersey, the island she had always loved. She was buried in St. Saviour's Churchyard, a marble bust on a granite base marking her grave and in the Church is a beautiful memorial tablet.

The *Jersey Lily* had returned home.

Lillie, playing a principal boy still on the stage in her early sixties.

Lillie in the year of her death (1929).

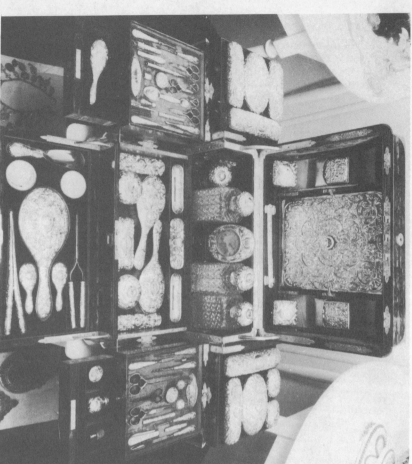

Lillie's travelling make-up case; this beautiful silver cabinet can now be seen in the Jersey museum.

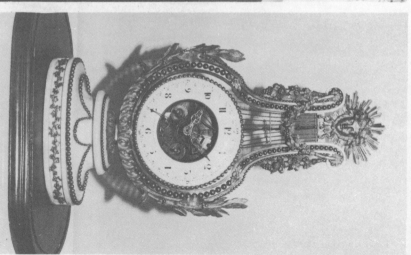

Clock left by Lillie to the Société Jersiaise, now to be seen in the Jersey museum.

THEATRE ROYAL

·HAYMARKET·

Licensed by the Lord Chamberlain to Mr. Bancroft, 18, Berkeley Square.

AREWELL ✦ PROGRAMME

ON THE OCCASION OF

MR. & MRS. BANCROFT'S

RETIREMENT

FROM

MANAGEMENT.

* * * * * * * *

MONDAY, JULY 20th, 1885.

* * * * * * * *

Barraud, Photo.   Oxford Street.

THEIR ROYAL HIGHNESSES

THE PRINCE AND PRINCESS OF WALES

Having Graciously Signified their Intention to be Present.

*Farewell Programme for the Bancrofts, whose photograph is actually stuck on.
Note Henry Irving's name in the top left hand corner who was appearing. Mrs.
Langtry played Georgina Vesey in "Money".*

The JERSEY LILY

HANHART LITH.

PolKa

BY

P. ROWE.

LONDON;
METZLER & C? 42 GREAT MARLBOROUGH S?W.

ENT. STA. HALL.

Price 4/-
Full Orchestra 2/6d
Septett 1/4 "
Brass Band 2 " "
Military " 5 "

56

DEDICATED (By Special Permission) TO Mrs LANGTRY.

"LILLIE"

✤ WALTZ. ✤

By permission from Copyright
Photograph by Van der Weyde.

"INK PHOTO". SPRAGUE & C?. LONDON.

BY

H. ELLIOT LATH.

(COMPOSER OF "HER MAJESTY'S" WALTZ, "EAST LYNNE" GAVOTTE; "LILLIE" WALTZ; "CÆSAREA" GAVOTTE;
"THE FORTESCUE" WALTZ; "FURORE" POLKA; ETC. ETC.)

ENT. STA. HALL

LONDON

PRICE _____ 2/-
DUET _____ 2/-
SEPTET _____ 1/-
FULL ORCHESTRA 1/6

THEATRE ROYAL.

Sole Proprietor and Manager, - - - - - - Mr. J. F. WARDEN.
Secretary and Business Manager, - - - - Mr. WM. BRICKWELL.

MR. WARDEN has much pleasure in announcing the Special Engagement for

Six Nights and One Grand Day Performance.

OF

Mrs. Langtry

ACCOMPANIED BY

⊹ MR. COGHLAN ⊹

And her own Company from the Prince's Theatre, London,

Commencing MONDAY, NOVEMBER 23rd, 1885.

| Stage Manager, | For | Mr. THOMAS COE |
| Business Manager, | MRS. LANGTRY | Mr. GEORGE KEOGH |

Doors Open at 7; Performance to commence at 7-30.

☞ NOTICE.—In consequence of the great expense attending this important engagement, the Prices
of Admission must of necessity be—

Balcony Stalls,	-	7s. 6d.
Orchestra Stalls,	-	5s. od.
Upper Circle,	-	4s. od.
Pit,	-	2s. od.
Gallery,	-	1s. od.

No Second Price.

Private Boxes to hold Three, 22s. 6d.; to hold Four, 30s.; to hold Five, 37s. 6d.; to hold Six, 45s.;
to hold Seven, 52s. 6d.; to hold Eight, 60s.

Box Office Open Daily from 10 till 3, where Seats to Balcony Stalls and Private Boxes may be secured for any night free of extra charge,
or by letter or telegram addressed to Mr. WM. BRICKWELL.

RAILWAY ARRANGEMENTS.

GREAT NORTHERN.—Late Trains every night during the week to Lisburn at 10-45, and on Wednesday to
Portadown at 10-45, calling at all stations except Lambeg.
NORTHERN COUNTIES.—Late Train every night during the week to Carrickfergus at 10-45, Friday at 11-0,
and on Thursday to Ballymena and Larne at 10-45, calling at all Stations.
COUNTY DOWN.—On Monday, Friday, and Saturday, to Newtownards at 11-0 p.m., calling at all Stations.
On Friday to Donaghadee, Downpatrick, and Ballynahinch, at 11-0 p.m., calling at all Stations.
HOLYWOOD & BANGOR.—Every night during the week to Bangor at 11-0, calling at all Stations.

DAVID ALLEN & SONS, Printers, 18, Corporation Street, Belfast.

Original programme of Theatre Royal, with Lillie in four plays; "Peril", "School for Scandal", "Lady of Lyons" and "She Stoops To Conquer".

58

LIVERPOOL

SHAKESPEARE THEATRE.

FRASER ST. LONDON RD.

Manager ... ... Mr. G. W. HARRIS
Treasurer ... Mr. JOHN GAFFNEY | Secretary ... Mr. B. HENDERSON HOWAT

SIX NIGHTS ONLY, commencing MONDAY, OCTOBER 5th, 1891.

MRS LANGTRY

General Manager for Mrs. Langtry (to whom all Business Communications should be addressed), MR E. B. NORMAN

GRAND PRODUQTION OF SHAKESPEARE'S

ANTONY AND CLEOPATRA

As played by Mrs Langtry and her Company for ninety-six performances at the Princess's Theatre, London.

MRS. LANGTRY AS "CLEOPATRA."

Princess's Theatre Company, Scenery and Costumes, Music by E. Jakobowski, Armour, Dances by D'Auban, Properties, Processions and Effects.

ANTONY & CLEOPATRA

DRAMATIS PERSONÆ.

Mark Antony, a Triumvir ... Mr FRANK WORTHING	Mardian, in attendance on Cleopatra Mr HARRY FENWICK
Octavius Cæsar, a Triumvir ... Mr WALTER GAY	Eutexena, Treasurer to Cleopatra ... Mr H. NORTON
M. Æmil. Lepidus, a Triumvir ... Mr ARTHUR COE	A Messenger ... ... Mr OSCAR ADYE
Sextus Pompeius ... ... Mr KENNETH BLACK	A Soothsayer ... ... Mr E. H. ALBERT
Domitius Enobarbus ... Mr FRED EVERILL	A Clown ... ... Mr F. NELSON
Ventidius ⎰ Friends of ⎱ Mr P. R. MACNAMARA	First Soldier ... ... Mr H. DANIELS
Eros ⎱ Antony ⎰ Mr ROLAND ATWOOD	Second Soldier ... ... Mr A. WATSON
Scarus ... Mr W. LOCKHART	Octavia, Sister of Cæsar and Wife of Antony
Mecænas ... ... Mr LIONEL BELMORE	... ... Miss ETHEL HOPE
Proculeius ⎰ Friends of Cæsar ⎱ Mr F. TEALE LINGHAM	Charmian ⎰ in attendance on ⎱ ... Miss AMY McNEILL
Thyreus ⎱ ⎰ Mr EDMUND S. EARLE	Iras ⎱ Cleopatra ⎰ ... Miss ADAH BARTON
Menas ⎰ Friends of ⎱ Mr G. WILLIAMS	Day ⎰ characters in the ⎱ ... Miss FANNY WRIGHT
Varrius ⎱ Pompey ⎰ Mr E. BROUGHTON	Night ⎱ Interlude ⎰ ... Miss LOUIE DALMOUR
Alexas, in attendance on Cleopatra ... Mr JOHN M. EAST	Cleopatra, Queen of Egypt ... Mrs LANGTRY

Officers, Soldiers, Messengers, Slaves, Peasants, and Dancers.

SYNOPSIS OF SCENERY.

SIX NIGHTS ONLY, commencing MONDAY, OCT. 5th, † 7-30.

Act 1. Scene 1. - - ATRIUM, IN CÆSAR'S HOUSE, ROME (Banks.)
Scene 2. Exterior of Cleopatra's Palace, Alexandria (Bruce Smith).
Scene 3. A Room in Pompey's House, Messina (Banks). Scene 4. Exterior of Cleopatra's Palace, Alexandria (Bruce Smith).

Act 2. Scene 1. - - ROME. AN OPEN PLACE (Perkins).
Scene 2. Atrium, in Cæsar's House, Rome (Banks). Scene 3. A Hall in Cleopatra's Palace, Alexandria (Harker).

Act 3. Scene 1. - - ATRIUM IN CÆSAR'S HOUSE, ROME (Banks).
Scene 2. The Open Country (Perkins).
Scene 3. A HALL IN CLEOPATRA'S PALACE, ALEXANDRIA (Harker)

ALEXANDRIAN FESTIVAL.

EGYPTIAN DANCE BY PRINCESS'S BALLET (Arranged by JOHN D'AUBAN)

Act 4. Scene 1 Under the Walls of Alexandria (Bruce Smith). Triumphal Reception of Antony by Cleopatra.
MARCH OF ROMAN LEGIONS. BACCHANTE DANCE (arranged by JOAN D'AUBAN). Revolving change to
Scene 2. OUTSIDE THE PALACE, ALEXANDRIA (Bruce Smith).

Act 5. Scene 1. Interior of an Egyptian Monument (Bruce Smith). MORNING.
The Original Music specially written for the Play by Mr. EDWARD JAKOBOWSKI ; the Triumphal March in Act IV. by Mr W. CORRI, June. Dances arranged by Mr JOHN D'AUBAN. The Magnificent Costumes by M. BIANCHINI ; LANDOLF ET CIE, Paris ; M. and Madame ALIAS, London. Armour by GUTPERLE ET CIE, Paris, and Messrs KENNEDY, Birmingham. Wigs by W. CLARKSON, 45, Wellington Street, Strand, London.

Monday, Oct. 12th, the wonderfully-successful Military Comedy, from the Globe Theatre, London,

BOOTLES' BABY

Musical Director ... ... Mr FRED WRIGHT | Chef de Foyer ... ... Mr W. SKAIFE

Doors open at 7-15, to commence at 7-30. Early Door open at 7 o'clock. 6d. Extra
☞ SPECIAL NOTICE.—In consequence of the Great Expense attendant upon this Engagement the PRICES OF ADMISSION for these Performances will be as follows:—

PRICES:—PRIVATE BOXES £2 12s. 6d., STALLS 6s. 6d., DRESS CIRCLE, 3s. 6d., PIT STALLS 2s. 6d. UPPER CIRCLE 1s. 6d. GALLERY, 6d. (Entrance Wilde Street)

PIT ONE SHILLING

SEATS NOT GUARANTEED. CHILDREN IN ARMS WILL NOT BE ADMITTED.
BOX OFFICE OPEN DAILY FROM 10 TO 4. TELEPHONE 1227

THE IMPERIAL THEATRE

Lessee and Manager .... Mrs. LANGTRY.

Every Evening at 8.15, and on Wednesday Afternoons at 2.30.

A ROYAL NECKLACE

By PIERRE and CLAUDE BERTON.

The Play produced by Mr. ARTHUR COE, under the direction of M. PIERRE FEWIER.

Marie Antoinette (Queen of France)	Mrs. LANGTRY	Duke de Lauzun	Mr. SCOTT CRAVEN
Mlle. Olive		Count de Polignac	Mr. DAVID GLASSFORD
Comtesse de la Motte	Miss CECIL RALEIGH	Colgny	Mr. JOSEPH WILSON
Comtesse de Polignac	Miss LILIAN BRAITHWAITE	Vaudreuil	Mr. W. T. STAVELEY
Duchess de Grammont	Miss INA GOLDSMITH	De Breteuil	Mr. W. CALVERT
Baroness de Mackau	Miss CYRIL WYNDE	Cangé (a Jeweller)	Mr. EDWARD FRECHER
Mlle. Bertin (Court Dressmaker)	Miss ETHEL WHITBURN	A Bookseller	Mr. W. GAVER MACKAY
A Strolling Danser	Miss MARIANNE CALDWELL	A Chestnut Seller	Mr. R. STANTON
A Flower-...	Miss LUCY MILNER	A Bystander	Mr. GEORGE LAUREY
The Dauphin	Miss WINNIE HALL	A Portrait Seller	Mr. ARTHUR BOUYER
Cross Patient	Mr. HUBERT TABER	A Spygrazil Boy	Miss ETHEL LEE
King Louis XVI.	Mr. CHARLES ALLAN	Lafette or otto Colin	Mr. SLEIGHT
Cardinal Rohan	Mr. EDMUND MAURICE	De Morri	Mr. POOLE
Count de la Motte	Mr. FULLER MELLISH	First Guide, Escort	Mr. HENRY CRISP
Bochmer (the Jeweller)	Mr. GILBERT FARQUHAR	Second Swiss Escort	Mr. AUBREY CHANDLER
Count Cagliostro	Mr. S. A. COOKSON	Sergt. La Rose	Mr. W. JOHNSTONE
Beaumou	Mr. THOMAS TERRISS	Officer of the Guard	Mr. HUBERT EVELYN
Patissau de Villette	Mr. SYDNEY LAWRENCE	Servant	Mr. EDWIN PALMER
Count de Provence ("Monsieur")	Mr. GEORGE HAWTREY		
Comte D'Artois	Mr. H. HASSARD-SHORT		

Court Ladies : Miss OCTAVIA KENWORTH, Miss SYBIL SHAKESPEAR, Miss VIOLET STUART, Miss OLIVE BLAIR, and Miss TINA DUVERY WARD.
Waiting Maids, Peasants, &c. : Miss GERTRUDE DE BEAUX, Miss MAUD BANNAR, Miss VICELLA, Miss MABEL ERDMAN, Miss DORIS WINDHAM, and Miss WILMOTT.
Courtiers, Priests, Pages, &c. : Messrs. FARQUE, KING, BENYHAM, COOKER, FAWN, DUFFLIN, BELLAMY, BEVON, and J. CAVE.
Soldiers, Street Boys, Street Hawkers, &c.

Synopsis of Scenery.

Act I. Sc. 1. Room in Count Cagliostro's House (Paris)
Sc. 2. A Street in Paris. Winter. (Joseph Harker)
Sc. 3. The Dauphin's Bedroom. Versailles.
(Joseph Harker)
Time—January and August, 1785.

Act II. The Park of Trianon, Versailles. Summer.
(W. Telbin)
Act III. The Queen's Salon, Versailles. (H. R. Browne)
Act IV. An Inn, Outside Versailles. (W. Telbin)

The Scenery in Act III. designed by Mr. FRANK VERITY. Furniture by H. NAYER & STEPHENSON, Ltd.

Intervals.

Between Scene 1 and Scene 2 of Act I., four minutes. Between Scenes 3 of Act I. and Act II., fifteen minutes.
Between Scene 2 and Acted 3 of Act I., three minutes. Between Acts II. and Act III., twelve minutes.
Between Act III. and Act IV., ten minutes.

Programme of Music.

OVERTURE	"Lucrezia"	Manon	Philo
AIRS DE BALLET		LE ROI D'AMONE (Bois de Dames dans la style ancien)	Massipol
		CANCONET ET NOUONI D'ALINE	Massipol

Incidental Music arranged by Mr. LEONARD CHALK.
The Incidental Songs in Act II., sung by Miss PHYLIS STRANGE.

Costumes designed and executed by M. BAIMULLOR of the National Opera, Paris ; also by M. WORTH of Paris, and Messrs. L. and D. NATHAN.
Wigs and Head-dresses by LEANDOR.
Electrical Effects by Messrs. VAUGHAN & BENCO. The Pearl arranged by M. FELIX BERTRAND.
The Scenes and Upholstery of the Auditorium by Messrs. L. R. LINING & CO., 25, St. Mary Axe, E.C.
Carpets by HAMPTON, LIMITED.

NO FEES. Attendants are forbidden to receive fees or charge money for programmes. Mrs. LANGTRY asks that visitors to the theatre will make free in reporting this regulation.

MATINÉES of A ROYAL NECKLACE on Wednesdays, at 2.30.

Stage Manager ...... Mr. T. MORRAY WALTER. Assistant Stage Manager ...... Mr. ARTHUR BOUYER.
Musical Director ...... Mr. LEONARD CHALK.
Acting Manager ...... Mr. FITZROY GARDNER.

On SATURDAY, SEPTEMBER 23rd, 1899,
Monday 25th, Tuesday 26th, Wednesday 27th, Thursday 28th, Friday 29th,
and Saturday, 30th, Shakespeare's Comedy,

AS YOU LIKE IT

Dramatis Personae.

Duke (living in exile)	...	Mr. WEATHERSBY
Amiens	Lords attending the banished Duke	Mr. COVENTRY
Jaques		Mr. J. G. GRAHAME
Duke Frederick (Brother of the banished Duke, and usurper of his dominions)		Mr. COE
Le Beau (a Courtier attending Frederick)	Mr. F. B. MARSHALL
Charles (the Wrestler)		Mr. H. CRISP
Touchstone (a Clown)		Mr. J. G. TAYLOR
Oliver	Sons of Sir Rowland de Boys	Mr. M. R. BELTEN
Jaques		Mr. WILLIAMS
Orlando		Mr. F. COOPER
Adam		Mr. E. SHEPHERD
Corin	Shepherds	Mr. J. W. PIGOTT
Sylvius		Mr. COLEMAN
William (a Country fellow, in love with Audrey)	Mr. HALL
Rosalind (Daughter of the banished Duke)	Mrs. LANGTRY
Celia (Daughter of Duke Frederick)	Miss KATE PATTISON
Phebe (a Shepherdess)	Miss ROSA KENNEY
Audrey (a Country Girl)	Miss KATE HODSON

SYNOPSIS OF SCENERY

Painted by Mr. ALFRED CRAVEN and Assistants.

ACT I.

SCENE 1.—OLIVER'S HOUSE AND ORCHARD.

Sc. 2. - Terrace & Garden of the Duke's Palace.

ACT II.

SCENE 1.—OLIVER'S HOUSE AND ORCHARD.

Sc. 2. - THE FOREST OF ARDEN.

SCENE 3. - ROAD LEADING TO THE FOREST.

SCENE 4.—SAME AS SCENE 2.

ACTS III., IV., & V.

SCENE. THE FOREST OF ARDEN.

All the Original Music and Glees will be given by a
specially selected Chorus under Mr. NOSAY ; and the Band
will be conducted by Mr. BARNARD. New Costumes by
Mr. STORCHURGHES. The Comedy produced under the super-
intendence of Mr. COE, Stage Manager.

60

A collection of original sepia prints and postcards
with two actually signed by Lillie.

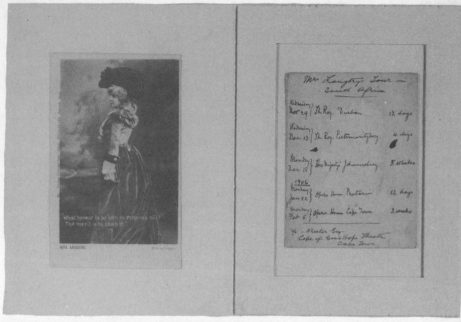

Details of Lillie's South African Tour 1905-1906.

An original letter from Lillie to a Mr. Finden; "Please come on Tuesday and see the alterations in Mlle. Mars as well as the first piece, I am having a hard struggle, I want a little help from my friends badly."

Pear's soap advertisements featuring Lillie and a recent mock-up advertisement using Francesca Annis, who played "Lillie" in the famous television series.

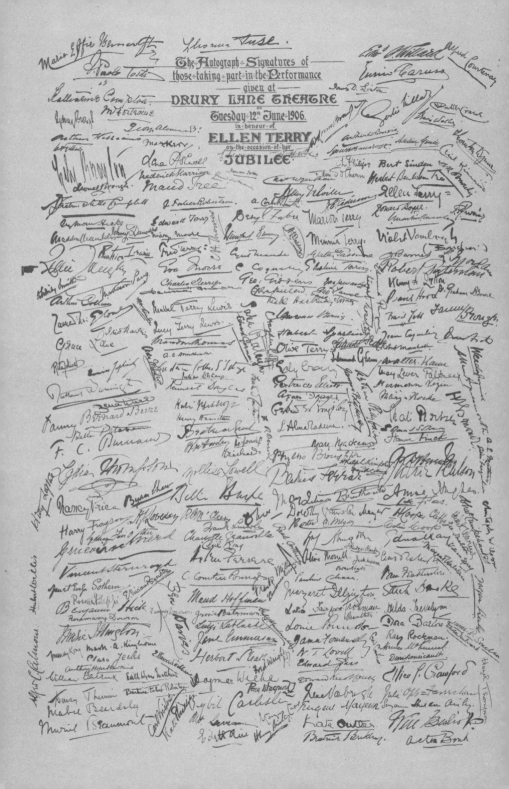

The Autograph Signatures of
those taking part in the Performance
given at
DRURY LANE THEATRE
on
Tuesday 12th June 1906.
in honour of
ELLEN TERRY
on the occasion of her
JUBILEE